CW00519425

Plant Based Diet

Cookbook

2021

How To Weight Loss And Stay Healthy With Plant Based Diet Lifestyle

Jennifer Smith

Table of Content

BREAKFAST 8

.... 8

EASY HUMMUS TOAST 9
PINEAPPLE AND KALE SMOOTHIE.. 10
CASHEW CHEESE SPREAD.. 11
VANILLA AND ALMOND SMOOTHIE... 12
NO-BAKE CHEWY GRANOLA BARS 13
HOT SAUSAGE AND PEPPER BREAKFAST CASSEROLE.................... 15
CARDAMOM & BLUEBERRY OATMEAL 18
HIGH PROTEIN PEANUT BUTTER SMOOTHIE 20
FLUFFY GARBANZO BEAN OMELET.. 22
CHILLED CANTALOUPE SMOOTHIE.. 24

MAINS 25

.... 25
VEGGIE & TOFU KEBABS.. 26
TANGY TOFU MEATLOAF.. 28
VEGAN BACON WRAPPED TOFU WITH BUTTERED SPINACH 30
SPANISH CHICKPEA SPINACH STEW 32
ROASTED VEGGIES IN LEMON SAUCE...................................... 34
TACO TEMPEH STUFFED PEPPERS 36
CARROT AND RADISH SLAW WITH SESAME DRESSING 38
SPICY SNOW PEA AND TOFU STIR FRY 40
POTATO BEAN QUESADILLAS.. 43
LENTILS SALAD WITH LEMON TAHINI DRESSING 45
LEMON PEPPER PASTA.. 47

SIDES AND SALADS 50

.... 50

KALE SALAD WITH TAHINI DRESSING 51
PENNE PASTA SALAD 54
ROASTED FENNEL SALAD.. 56

BROCCOLI SWEET POTATO CHICKPEA SALAD 58

SOUPS AND STEWS 60

.... 60

CURRIED CARROT KALE SOUP...61
LENTIL AND MIXED VEGETABLE SOUP 63
TURNIP–TOMATO SOUP 65
CHILLED LEMONGRASS AND AVOCADO SOUP..............................67
BROCCOLI AND COLLARD SOUP...68
PUMPKIN STEW..70
SPRING VEGETABLE SOUP 72
BEAN ONION STEW...74

SAUCES, AND CONDIMENTS 75

NACHO CHEESE SAUCE...75
THAI PEANUT SAUCE 76
GARLIC ALFREDO SAUCE 79
CASHEW YOGURT..81

SNACKS 83

ARTICHOKES WITH MAYO SAUCE 83
EGGPLANT AND ZUCCHINI SNACK..85
MUSHROOM STUFFED POBLANO 87
FRIED MUSTARD GREENS..89
CHEESE BRUSSELS SPROUTS 91

DESSERTS AND DRINKS... 93

.... 93

PEACH POPSICLES...94
PROTEIN FAT BOMBS 96
COCONUT FAT BOMBS..98
CHOCOLATE PEANUT FAT BOMBS...99
APPLE PIE BITES 101
MOJITO FAT BOMBS 103

BREAKFAST

Easy Hummus Toast

Preparation time: 10 minutes

Cooking Time 0 minutes

Servings 1

Ingredients

- 2 slices sprouted wheat bread
- ¼ cup hummus
- 1 tablespoon hemp seeds
- 1 tablespoon roasted unsalted sunflower seeds

Directions:

1. Start by toasting your bread.
2. Top with the hummus and seeds then eat!

Nutrition:

Calories 445, Total Fat 16.3g, Saturated Fat 2.2g, Cholesterol 0mg, Sodium 597mg, Total Carbohydrate 54.5g, Dietary Fiber 10.5g, Total Sugars 6.1g, Protein 22.6g, Calcium 116mg, Iron 6mg, Potassium 471mg

Pineapple and Kale Smoothie

Preparation time: 3 minutes

Servings 2

Ingredients

- 1 cup Greek yogurt
- 1½ cups cubed pineapple
- 3 cups baby kale
- 1 cucumber
- 2 tbsp, hemp seeds

Directions:

1. Pop everything in a blender and blitz
2. Pour into glasses and serve.

Nutrition:

Calories 509, Total Fat 8.9g, Saturated Fat 3.3g, Cholesterol 10mg, Sodium 127mg, Total Carbohydrate 87.1g, Dietary Fiber 10.3g, Total Sugars 55.3g, Protein 30.6g, Vitamin D 0mcg, Calcium 438mg, Iron 5mg, Potassium 1068mg

Cashew Cheese Spread

Preparation Time: 5 minutes

Cooking Time: 0 minutes

Servings: 5

Ingredients:

- 1 cup water
- 1 cup raw cashews
- 1 tsp. nutritional yeast
- ½ tsp. salt

Optional: 1 tsp. garlic powder

Directions:

1. Soak the cashews for 6 hours in water.
2. Drain and transfer the soaked cashews to a food processor.
3. Add 1 cup of water and all the other ingredients and blend.
4. For the best flavor, serve chilled.
5. Enjoy immediately, or store for later.

Nutrition:

Calories 162, Total Fat 12.7g, Saturated Fat 2.5g, Cholesterol 0mg, Sodium 239mg, Total Carbohydrate 9.7g, Dietary Fiber 1.1g, Total Sugars 1.5g, Protein 4.6g, Calcium 15mg, Iron 2mg, Potassium 178mg

Vanilla and Almond Smoothie

Preparation time: 3 minutes

Servings 1

Ingredients

- 2 scoops vegan vanilla protein powder
- ½ cup almonds
- 1 cup water

Directions:

1. Pop everything in a blender and blitz
2. Pour into glasses and serve.

Nutrition:

Calories 415, Total Fat 33.8g, Saturated Fat 1.8g, Cholesterol 0mg, Sodium 108mg, Total Carbohydrate 18.2g, Dietary Fiber 7.9g, Total Sugars 2g, Protein 42.1g, Vitamin D 0mcg, Calcium 255mg, Iron 9mg, Potassium 351mg

No-Bake Chewy Granola Bars

Preparation time: 10 minutes

Cooking Time 10 minutes

Servings 8

Ingredients

- ¼ cup coconut oil
- ¼ cup honey or maple syrup
- ¼ teaspoon salt
- 1 teaspoon vanilla extract
- ½ teaspoon cardamominutes
- ¼ teaspoon cinnamon
- Pinch of nutmeg
- 1 cup old-fashioned oats
- ½ cup sliced raw almonds
- ¼ cup sunflower seeds
- ¼ cup pumpkin seeds
- 1 tablespoon chia seeds
- 1 cup chopped dried figs

Directions:

1. Line a 6" x 8" baking dish with parchment paper and pop to one side.
2. Grab a saucepan and add the oil, honey, salt and spices.
3. Pop over a medium heat and stir until it melts together.
4. Reduce the heat, add the oats and stir to coat.

5. Add the seeds, nuts and dried fruit and stir through again.

6. Cooking Time: for 10 minutes.

7. Remove from the heat and transfer the oat mixture to the pan.

8. Press down until it's packed firm.

9. Leave to cool completely then cut into 8 bars.

10. Serve and enjoy.

Nutrition:

Calories 243, Total Fat 13.3g, Saturated Fat 6.7g, Cholesterol 0mg, Sodium 78mg, Total Carbohydrate 30.8g, Dietary Fiber 4.3g, Total Sugars 21.1g, Protein 4.2g, Calcium 67mg, Iron 2mg, Potassium 285mg

Hot Sausage and Pepper Breakfast Casserole

Preparation time: 57 minutes

Cooking Time 50 minutes

Servings 8

Ingredients

- 10 cup white bread, cubed
- 2¾ cups ice water
- 1 ¼ cup plant-based unsweetened creamer
- 2 tablespoons extra-virgin olive oil
- 3 vegan sausage, sliced
- 1 bell pepper, seeded and chopped
- 1 medium onion, chopped
- 2 garlic cloves, minced
- 5 cups spinach leaves
- 1 cup vegan parmesan, grated
- 1 teaspoon ground sea salt, or to taste
- ½ teaspoon ground nutmeg
- ½ teaspoon ground black pepper
- 1 tablespoon fresh parsley, chopped
- 1 teaspoon fresh rosemary, chopped
- 1 teaspoon fresh thyme, chopped
- 1 teaspoon fresh oregano, chopped
- 1 tablespoon vegan butter

Directions:

1. Preheat your oven to 375°F and grease a 13" x 8" baking dish.
2. Grab a medium bowl and add the water, milk and nutmeg. Whisk well until combined.
3. Pop a skillet over a medium heat and add the oil.
4. Add the sausage to the pan and Cooking Time: for 8-10 minutes until browned. Remove from the pan and pop to one side.
5. Add the onions and Cooking Time: for 3 minutes.
6. Add the peppers and Cooking Time: for 5 minutes.
7. Add the garlic, salt and pepper and Cooking Time: for 2 minutes then remove from the pan and pop to one side.
8. Add the spinach to the pan and Cooking Time: until wilted.
9. Remove the spinach from the pan then chop. Squeeze out the water.
10. Grab the greased baking dish and add half the cubed bread to the bottom.
11. Add half the spinach to the top followed by half the spinach and half of the onion and pepper mixture.
12. Sprinkle with half the parmesan then repeat.
13. Whisk the egg mixture again then pour over the casserole.
14. Pop into the oven and bake for 30 minutes until browned.
15. Serve and enjoy.

Nutrition:

Calories 263, Total Fat 8.2g, Saturated Fat 1g, Cholesterol 0mg, Sodium 673mg, Total Carbohydrate 31.8g, Dietary Fiber 3.4g, Total Sugars 3.6g, Protein 12.9g, Calcium 239mg, Iron 3mg, Potassium 377mg

Cardamom & Blueberry Oatmeal

Preparation time: 10 minutes

Cooking Time 3 minutes

Servings 1

Ingredients

- ¾ cup quick oats
- 1¼ cup water
- ½ cup unsweetened almond milk, divided
- 2 tablespoons pure maple syrup
- ¼ heaping teaspoon cinnamon
- 1/8 teaspoon cardamominutes
- Handful walnuts
- Handful dried currants

Directions:

1. Place the water into a small saucepan and bring to the boil.
2. Add the oats, stir through, reduce the heat to medium and Cooking Time: for 3 minutes.
3. Add half of the milk, stir again and Cooking Time: for another few seconds.
4. Remove from the heat and leave to stand for 3 minutes.
5. Transfer to a bowl and to with the remaining ingredients.
6. Drizzle with the milk then serve and enjoy.

Nutrition:

Calories 568, Total Fat 24.4g, Saturated Fat 1.9g, Cholesterol 0mg, Sodium 118mg, Total Carbohydrate 77g, Dietary Fiber 10.4g, Total Sugars 26.8g, Protein 16.5g, Vitamin D 1mcg, Calcium 263mg, Iron 5mg, Potassium 651mg

High Protein Peanut Butter Smoothie

Preparation time: 3 minutes

Servings: 2

Ingredients

- 2 cups kale
- 1 banana
- 2 tbsp. hemp seeds
- 1 tbsp. peanut butter
- 2/3 cup water
- 2 cups ice
- 1 cup almond or cashew milk
- 2 tbsp. cacao powder
- 1 scoop Vega vanilla protein powder

Directions:

1. Pop the kale and banana in a blender, then add the hemp seeds and peanut butter.
2. Add the milk, water and ice and blend until ingredients are combined.
3. Add the protein powder.
4. Pour into glasses and serve.

Nutrition:

Calories 687, Total Fat 50.4g, Saturated Fat 38g, Cholesterol 0mg, Sodium 176mg, Total Carbohydrate 46.5g, Dietary Fiber 9.9g, Total Sugars 23.7g, Protein 20.4g, Vitamin D 0mcg, Calcium 150mg, Iron 8mg, Potassium 979mg

Fluffy Garbanzo Bean Omelet

Preparation time: 20 minutes

Cooking Time 7 minutes

Servings 2

Ingredients

- ¼ cup besan flour
- 1 tablespoon nutritional yeast
- ½ teaspoon baking powder
- ¼ teaspoon turmeric
- ½ teaspoon chopped chives
- ¼ teaspoon garlic powder
- 1/8 teaspoon black pepper
- ½ teaspoon Ener-G egg replacer
- ¼ cup water
- ½ cup Romaine Leafy Green Fresh Express
- ½ cup Veggies
- 1 tablespoon Salsa
- 1 tablespoon Ketchup
- 1 tablespoon Hot sauce
- 1 tablespoon Parsley

Directions:

1. Grab a medium bowl and combine all the ingredients except the greens and veggies. Leave to stand for five minutes.

2. Place a skillet over a medium heat and add the oil.

3. Pour the batter into the pan, spread and Cooking Time: for 3-5 minutes until the edges pull away from the pan.

4. Add the greens and the veggies of your choice then fold the omelet over.

5. Cooking Time: for 2 more minutes then pop onto a plate.

6. Serve with the topping of your choice.

7. Serve and enjoy.

Nutrition:

Calories 104, Total Fat 1.3g, Saturated Fat 0.2g, Cholesterol 0mg, Sodium 419mg, Total Carbohydrate 17.9g, Dietary Fiber 4.6g, Total Sugars 4.7g, Protein 6.6g, Calcium 69mg, Iron 3mg, Potassium 423mg

Chilled Cantaloupe Smoothie

Preparation time: 10 minutes

Servings 2

Ingredients:

- 1½ cups cantaloupe, diced
- 2 Tbsp frozen orange juice concentrate
- ¼ cup white wine
- 2 ice cubes
- 1 Tbsp lemon juice
- ½ cup Mint leaves, for garnish

Directions:

1. Blend all ingredients to create a smooth mixture.
2. Top with mint leaves, and serve.

Nutrition:

Calories 349, Total Fat 13.1g, Saturated Fat 11.3g, Cholesterol 0mg, Sodium 104mg, Total Carbohydrate 50.5g, Dietary Fiber 5.5g, Total Sugars 46.4g, Protein 6.5g, Vitamin D 0mcg, Calcium 117mg, Iron 5mg, Potassium 1320mg

MAINS

Veggie & Tofu Kebabs

Preparation Time: 15 minutes

Cooking Time: 12 minutes

Servings: 4

Ingredients:

- 2 cloves garlic, minced
- ¼ cup balsamic vinegar
- ¼ cup olive oil
- 1 tablespoon Italian seasoning
- Salt and pepper to taste
- 1 onion, sliced into quarters
- 12 medium mushrooms
- 16 cherry tomatoes
- 1 zucchini, sliced into rounds
- 1 cup tofu, cubed
- 4 cups cauliflower rice

Directions:

1. In a bowl, mix the garlic, vinegar, oil, Italian seasoning, salt and pepper.
2. Toss the vegetable slices and tofu in the mixture.
3. Marinate for 1 hour.
4. Thread into 8 skewers and grill for 12 minutes, turning once or twice.
5. Add cauliflower rice into 4 food containers.

6. Add 2 kebab skewers on top of each container of cauliflower rice.

7. Reheat kebabs in the grill before serving.

Nutritional Value:

Calories 58

Total Fat 2 g

Saturated Fat 0 g

Cholesterol 0 mg

Sodium 84 mg

Total Carbohydrate 9 g

Dietary Fiber 2 g

Total Sugars 5 g

Protein 2 g

Potassium 509 mg

Tangy Tofu Meatloaf

Preparation Time: 10 minutes

Cooking Time: 40 minutes

Servings: 6

Ingredients:

- 2 ½ lb ground tofu
- Salt and ground black pepper to taste
- 3 tbsp flaxseed meal
- 2 large eggs
- 2 tbsp olive oil
- 1 lemon,1 tbsp juiced
- ¼ cup freshly chopped parsley
- ¼ cup freshly chopped oregano
- 4 garlic cloves, minced
- Lemon slices to garnish

Directions:

1. Preheat the oven to 400 F and grease a loaf pan with cooking spray. Set aside.
2. In a large bowl, combine the tofu, salt, black pepper, and flaxseed meal. Set aside.
3. In a small bowl, whisk the eggs with the olive oil, lemon juice, parsley, oregano, and garlic. Pour the mixture onto the mix and combine well.
4. Spoon the tofu mixture into the loaf pan and press to fit into the pan. Bake in the middle rack of the oven for 30

to 40 minutes.

5. Remove the pan, tilt to drain the meat's liquid, and allow cooling for 5 minutes.

6. Slice, garnish with some lemon slices and serve with braised green beans.

Nutrition:

Calories:238, Total Fat:26.3g, Saturated Fat:14.9g, Total Carbs:1g, Dietary Fiber:0g, Sugar:0g, Protein:1g, Sodium:183mg

Vegan Bacon Wrapped Tofu With Buttered Spinach

Preparation Time: 5 minutes

Cooking Time: 20 minutes

Servings: 4

Ingredients:

For the bacon wrapped tofu:

- 4 tofu
- 8 slices vegan bacon
- Salt and black pepper to taste
- 2 tbsp olive oil

For the buttered spinach:

- 2 tbsp butter
- 1 lb spinach
- 4 garlic cloves
- Salt and ground black pepper to taste

Directions:

For the bacon wrapped tofu:

1. Preheat the oven to 450 F.
2. Wrap each tofu with two vegan bacon slices, season with salt and black pepper, and place on the baking sheet. Drizzle with the olive oil and bake in the oven for 15 minutes or until the vegan bacon browns and the tofu cooks within.

For the buttered spinach:

1. Meanwhile, melt the butter in a large skillet, add and sauté the spinach and garlic until the leaves wilt, 5 minutes. Season with salt and black pepper.
2. Remove the tofu from the oven and serve with the buttered spinach.

Nutrition:

Calories:260, Total Fat:24.7g, Saturated Fat:14.3g, Total Carbs:4g, Dietary Fiber:0g, Sugar:2g, Protein:6g, Sodium:215mg

Spanish Chickpea Spinach Stew

Preparation time: 10 minutes

Cooking time: 25 minutes

Servings: 4

Ingredients:

- 1 splash olive oil
- 1 small onion, chopped
- 2 cloves garlic
- 5g cumin powder
- 5g smoked paprika
- ¼ teaspoon chili powder
- 235ml water
- 670g can diced tomatoes
- 165g cooked chickpeas (or can chickpeas
- 60g baby spinach
- Salt, to taste
- A handful of chopped coriander, to garnish
- 20g slivered almonds, to garnish
- 4 slices toasted whole-grain bread, to serve with

Directions:

1. Heat olive oil in a saucepan over medium-high heat.
2. Add onion and Cooking Time: until browned, for 7-8 minutes.
3. Add garlic, cumin, paprika, and chili powder.

4. Cooking Time: 1 minute.

5. Add water and scrape any browned bits.

6. Add the tomatoes and chickpeas. Season to taste and reduce heat.

7. Simmer the soup for 10 minutes.

8. Stir in spinach and Cooking Time: 2 minutes.

9. Ladle soup in a bowl. Sprinkle with cilantro and almonds.

10. Serve with toasted bread slices.

Nutrition:

Calories 369

Total Fat 9.7g

Total Carbohydrate 67.9g

Dietary Fiber 19.9g

Total Sugars 13.9g

Protein 18g

Roasted Veggies In Lemon Sauce

Preparation Time: 15 minutes

Cooking Time: 20 minutes

Servings: 5

Ingredients:

- 2 cloves garlic, sliced
- 1 ½ cups broccoli florets
- 1 ½ cups cauliflower florets
- 1 tablespoon olive oil
- Salt to taste
- 1 teaspoon dried oregano, crushed
- ¾ cup zucchini, diced
- ¾ cup red bell pepper, diced
- 2 teaspoons lemon zest

Directions:

1. Preheat your oven to 425 degrees F.
2. In a baking pan, add the garlic, broccoli and cauliflower.
3. Toss in oil and season with salt and oregano.
4. Roast in the oven for 10 minutes.
5. Add the zucchini and bell pepper to the pan.
6. Stir well.
7. Roast for another 10 minutes.
8. Sprinkle lemon zest on top before serving.

9. Transfer to a food container and reheat before serving.

Nutritional Value:

Calories 52

Total Fat 3 g

Saturated Fat 0 g

Cholesterol 0 mg

Sodium 134 mg

Total Carbohydrate 5 g

Dietary Fiber 2 g

Total Sugars 2 g

Protein 2 g

Potassium 270 mg

Taco Tempeh Stuffed Peppers

Preparation Time: 15 minutes

Cooking Time: 41 minutes

Servings: 6

Ingredients:

- 6 yellow bell peppers, halved and deseeded
- 1 ½ tbsp olive oil
- Salt and ground black pepper to taste
- 3 tbsp butter
- 3 garlic cloves, minced
- ½ white onion, chopped
- 2 lbs. ground tempeh
- 3 tsp taco seasoning
- 1 cup riced broccoli
- ¼ cup grated cheddar cheese
- Plain unsweetened yogurt for serving

Directions:

1. Preheat the oven to 400 F and grease a baking dish with cooking spray. Set aside.
2. Drizzle the bell peppers with the olive oil and season with some salt. Set aside.
3. Melt the butter in a large skillet and sauté the garlic and onion for 3 minutes. Stir in the tempeh, taco seasoning, salt, and black pepper. Cooking Time: until the meat is

no longer pink, 8 minutes.

4. Mix in the broccoli until adequately incorporated. Turn the heat off.

5. Spoon the mixture into the peppers, top with the cheddar cheese, and place the peppers in the baking dish. Bake in the oven until the cheese melts and is bubbly, 30 minutes.

6. Remove the dish from the oven and plate the peppers. Top with the palin yogurt and serve warm.

Nutrition:

Calories:251, Total Fat:22.5g, Saturated Fat:3.8g, Total Carbs:13g, Dietary Fiber:9g, Sugar:2g, Protein:3g, Sodium:23mg

Carrot And Radish Slaw With Sesame Dressing

Preparation Time: 10 minutes

Cooking Time: 0 minute

Servings: 4

Ingredients:

- 2 tablespoons sesame oil, toasted
- 3 tablespoons rice vinegar
- ½ teaspoon sugar
- 2 tablespoons low sodium tamari
- 1 cup carrots, sliced into strips
- 2 cups radishes, sliced
- 2 tablespoons fresh cilantro, chopped
- 2 teaspoons sesame seeds, toasted

Directions:

1. Mix the oil, vinegar, sugar and tamari in a bowl.
2. Add the carrots, radishes and cilantro.
3. Toss to coat evenly.
4. Let sit for 10 minutes.
5. Transfer to a food container.

Nutritional Value:

Calories 98

Total Fat 8 g

Saturated Fat 1 g

Cholesterol 0 mg

Sodium 336 mg

Total Carbohydrate 6 g

Dietary Fiber 2 g

Total Sugars 3 g

Protein 2 g

Potassium 241 mg

Spicy Snow Pea And Tofu Stir Fry

Preparation Time: 20 minutes

Cooking Time: 20 minutes

Servings: 4

Ingredients:

- 1 cup unsalted natural peanut butter
- 2 teaspoons brown sugar
- 2 tablespoons reduced-sodium soy sauce
- 2 teaspoons hot sauce
- 3 tablespoons rice vinegar
- 14 oz. tofu
- 4 teaspoons oil
- 1/4 cup onion, sliced
- 2 tablespoons ginger, grated
- 3 cloves garlic, minced
- 1/2 cup broccoli, sliced into florets
- 1/2 cup carrot, sliced into sticks
- 2 cups fresh snow peas, trimmed
- 2 tablespoons water
- 2 cups brown rice, cooked
- 4 tablespoons roasted peanuts (unsalted

Directions:

1. In a bowl, mix the peanut butter, sugar, soy sauce, hot sauce and rice vinegar.

2. Blend until smooth and set aside.

3. Drain the tofu and sliced into cubes.

4. Pat dry with paper towel.

5. Add oil to a pan over medium heat.

6. Add the tofu and Cooking Time: for 2 minutes or until brown on all sides.

7. Transfer the tofu to a plate.

8. Add the onion, ginger and garlic to the pan.

9. Cooking Time: for 2 minutes.

10. Add the broccoli and carrot.

11. Cooking Time: for 5 minutes.

12. Stir in the snow peas.

13. Pour in the water and cover.

14. Cooking Time: for 4 minutes.

15. Add the peanut sauce to the pan along with the tofu.

16. Heat through for 30 seconds.

17. In a food container, add the brown rice and top with the tofu and vegetable stir fry.

18. Top with roasted peanuts.

Nutritional Value:

Calories 514

Total Fat 27 g

Saturated Fat 4 g

Cholesterol 0 mg

Sodium 376 mg

Total Carbohydrate 49 g

Dietary Fiber 7 g

Total Sugars 12 g

Protein 22 g

Potassium 319 mg

Potato Bean Quesadillas

Preparation time: 10 minutes

Cooking time: 10 minutes

Servings: 4

Ingredients:

- 4 whole-wheat tortillas
- 2 potatoes, boiled, cubed
- 200g refried beans
- 1 teaspoon chili powder
- ½ teaspoon dried oregano
- ¼ teaspoon garlic powder
- 120g spinach
- 1 onion, thinly sliced
- 2 cloves garlic, minced
- 30ml tamari sauce
- 45g nutritional yeast
- Salt and pepper, to taste

Directions:

1. Heat a splash of olive oil in a skillet.
2. Add onion and Cooking Time: over medium heat for 10 minutes, or until the onion is caramelized.
3. Add the garlic and Cooking Time: 1 minute.
4. Add spinach and toss gently.
5. Add tamari sauce and Cooking Time: 1 minutes.

6. Reheat the refried beans with nutritional yeast, chili, oregano, and garlic powder, in a microwave, on high for 1 minute.
7. Mash the potatoes and spread over tortilla.
8. Top the mashed potatoes with spinach mixture and refried beans.
9. Season to taste and place another tortilla on top.
10. Heat large skillet over medium-high heat.
11. Heat the tortilla until crispy. Flip and heat the other side.
12. Cut the tortilla in half and serve.

Nutrition:

Calories 232

Total Fat 2.1g

Total Carbohydrate 44.2g

Dietary Fiber 10.4g

Total Sugars 3g

Protein 12.4g

Lentils Salad With Lemon Tahini Dressing

Preparation time: 10 minutes

Cooking time: 30 minutes

Servings: 4

Ingredients:

- 225g green lentils, picked, rinsed
- 1 clove garlic, minced
- ¼ teaspoon ground cumin
- 5ml olive oil
- 1 red onion, finely diced
- 75g dried apricots, chopped
- 1 small red bell pepper, seeded, chopped
- 1 small green bell pepper, seeded, chopped
- 1 small yellow bell pepper, seeded, chopped
- 1 small cucumber, diced
- 20g sunflower seeds
- Salt and pepper, to taste

Lemon dressing:

- 1 lemon, juiced
- 30g tahini
- 5g chopped coriander
- Salt, to taste

Directions:

1. Place rinsed lentils in a saucepan.

2. Add enough water to cover.

3. Bring to a boil and skim off any foam. Add garlic and cumin.

4. Reduce heat and simmer the lentils for 30 minutes.

5. In the meantime, make the dressing by combining all the ingredients together.

6. Heat olive oil in a skillet. Add onion and bell peppers. Cooking Time: stirring over medium-high heat for 5 minutes.

7. Remove from the heat.

8. Drain the lentils and toss in a large bowl with the cooked vegetables, apricots, cucumber, and sunflower seeds. Season to taste.

9. Drizzle with dressing and serve.

Nutrition:

Calories 318

Total Fat 7g

Total Carbohydrate 49.2g

Dietary Fiber 20.8g

Total Sugars 7.9g

Protein 18.1g

Lemon Pepper Pasta

Preparation time: 5 minutes

Cooking time: 20 minutes

Servings: 4

Ingredients:

- 300g pasta, any kind, without eggs
- 400ml unsweetened soy milk
- 100g soy cream cheese
- 45g blanched almonds
- 45g nutritional yeast
- 1 teaspoon lemon zest, finely grated
- ¼ teaspoon lemon pepper
- 30ml olive oil
- 2 clove garlic, minced
- 5 capers, rinsed, chopped
- 10g parsley, chopped

Directions:

1. Cooking Time: the pasta, according to the package directions, in a pot filled with salted boiling water.
2. Strain the pasta and reserve 230ml cooking liquid.
3. Combine soy milk, soy cheese, almonds, nutritional yeast, lemon zest, and pepper lemon in a food blender.
4. Blend until smooth. Place aside.
5. Heat olive oil in a skillet.

6. Add the garlic, and Cooking Time: until very fragrant, for 1 minute.
7. Pour in the soy milk mixture and reserved pasta cooking liquid.
8. Bring to a boil, and reduce heat.
9. Stir in chopped capers and simmer 6-8 minutes or until creamy. Remove from the heat and stir in cooked pasta.
10. Toss the pasta gently to coat with the sauce.
11. Serve pasta, garnished with chopped parsley.

Nutrition:

Calories 489

Total Fat 23g

Total Carbohydrate 53.5g

Dietary Fiber 5.9g

Total Sugars 2.4g

Protein 20.4g

SIDES AND SALADS

Kale Salad With Tahini Dressing

Preparation time: 10 minutes

Cooking time: 20 minutes

Total time: 30 minutes

Servings: 04

Ingredients:

Roasted vegetables:

- 1 medium zucchini, chopped
- 1 medium sweet potato, chopped
- 1 cup red cabbage, chopped
- 1 tablespoon melted coconut oil
- 1 pinch salt
- ½ teaspoon curry powder

Dressing:

- ⅓ cup tahini
- ½ teaspoon garlic powder
- 1 tablespoon coconut aminos
- 1 pinch salt
- 1 large clove garlic, minced
- ¼ cup water

Salad:

- 6 cups mixed greens
- 4 small radishes, sliced
- 3 tablespoons hemp seeds

- 2 tablespoons lemon juice
- ½ ripe avocado, to garnish
- 2 tablespoons vegan feta cheese, crumbled
- Pomegranate seeds, to garnish
- Pecans, to garnish

How to Prepare:

1. Preheat your oven at 375 degrees F.
2. On a greased baking sheet, toss zucchini, sweet potato, and red cabbage with salt, curry powder, and oil.
3. Bake the zucchini cabbage mixture for 20 minutes in the oven.
4. Combine all the dressing ingredients in a small bowl.
5. In a salad bowl, toss in all the vegetables, roasted vegetables, and dressing.
6. Mix them well then refrigerate to chill.
7. Garnish with feta cheese, pecans, pomegranate seeds and avocado.
8. Serve.

Nutritional Values:

Calories 201

Total Fat 8.9 g

Saturated Fat 4.5 g

Cholesterol 57 mg

Sodium 340 mg

Total Carbs 24.7 g

Fiber 1.2 g

Sugar 1.3 g

Protein 15.3 g

Penne Pasta Salad

Preparation time: 30 minutes

Cooking time: 0 minutes

Total time: 30 minutes

Servings: 04

Ingredients:

Salad:

- 2 cups roasted tomatoes
- 12 ounces penne pasta

Pesto:

- 2 cups fresh basil
- 4 cloves garlic, minced
- ¼ cup toasted pine nuts
- 1 medium lemon, juice
- ¼ cup vegan cheese, shredded
- 1 pinch salt
- ¼ cup olive oil

How to Prepare:

1. In a blender, add all the pesto ingredients.
2. Blend them well until it is lump free.
3. In a salad bowl toss in pasta, roasted tomatoes, and pesto.
4. Mix them well then refrigerate to chill.
5. Serve.

Nutritional Values:

Calories 361

Total Fat 16.3 g

Saturated Fat 4.9 g

Cholesterol 114 mg

Sodium 515 mg

Total Carbs 29.3 g

Fiber 0.1 g

Sugar 18.2 g

Protein 3.3 g

Roasted Fennel Salad

Preparation time: 10 minutes

Cooking time: 20 minutes

Total time: 30 minutes

Servings: 4

Ingredients:

Fennel:

- 1 bulb fennel fronds, sliced
- 1 tablespoon curry powder
- 1 tablespoon avocado oil
- 1 pinch salt

Salad:

- 5 cups salad greens
- 1 red bell pepper, sliced

Dressing:

- ¼ cup tahini
- 1½ tablespoons lemon juice
- 1½ teaspoons apple cider vinegar
- 1 tablespoon freshly minced rosemary
- 3 cloves garlic, minced
- 1½ tablespoons coconut aminos
- 5 tablespoons water to thin
- 1 pinch salt

How to Prepare:

1. Preheat your oven at 375 degrees F.
2. On a greased baking sheet, toss fennel with salt, curry powder, and oil.
3. Bake the curried fennel for 20 minutes in the oven.
4. Combine all the dressing ingredients in a small bowl.
5. In a salad bowl, toss in all the vegetables, roasted fennel, and dressing.
6. Mix them well then refrigerate to chill.
7. Serve.

Nutritional Values:

Calories 205

Total Fat 22.7 g

Saturated Fat 6.1 g

Cholesterol 4 mg

Sodium 227 mg

Total Carbs 26.1 g

Fiber 1.4 g

Sugar 0.9 g

Protein 5.2 g

Broccoli Sweet Potato Chickpea Salad

Preparation time: 10 minutes

Cooking time: 22 minutes

Total time: 32 minutes

Servings: 06

Ingredients:

Vegetables:

- 1 large sweet potato, peeled and diced
- 1 head broccoli
- 2 tablespoons olive or grapeseed oil
- 1 pinch each salt and black pepper
- 1 teaspoon dried dill
- 1 medium red bell pepper

Chickpeas:

- 1 (15 ouncecan chickpeas, drained
- 1 tablespoon olive or grapeseed oil
- 1 tablespoon tandoori masala spice
- 1 pinch salt
- 1 teaspoon coconut sugar
- 1 pinch cayenne pepper

Garlic dill sauce:

- ⅓ cup hummus
- 3 large cloves garlic, minced
- 1 teaspoon dried dill

- 2 tablespoons lemon juice
- Water

How to Prepare:

1. Preheat your oven to 400 degrees F.
2. In a greased baking sheet, toss sweet potato with salt and oil.
3. Bake the sweet potatoes for 15 minutes in the oven.
4. Toss all chickpea ingredients and spread in a tray.
5. Bake them for 7 minutes in the oven.
6. Combine all the sauce ingredients in a small bowl.
7. In a salad bowl, toss in all the vegetables, roasted potato, chickpeas, and sauce.
8. Mix them well then refrigerate to chill.
9. Serve.

Nutritional Values:

Calories 231

Total Fat 20.1 g

Saturated Fat 2.4 g

Cholesterol 110 mg

Sodium 941 mg

Total Carbs 20.1 g

Fiber 0.9 g

Sugar 1.4 g

Protein 4.6 g

SOUPS AND STEWS

Curried Carrot Kale Soup

Preparation Time: 40 Minutes

Servings: 2

Ingredients:

- 2 cups kale, finely chopped (frozen or fresh
- 8 carrots, chopped
- 5 potatoes, chopped
- ½ yellow onion, chopped
- 3 garlic cloves, minced
- ¼ cup peanut butter, powdered
- 1 tsp cayenne pepper
- 1 tbsp curry powder
- 4 cups water
- 2 tsp of vegetable base (or use 2 cups water with 2 cups veggie broth

Directions:

1. Add garlic and onion to Instant Pot along with ¼ cup water and Switch on 'Sautée' button. Sauté garlic and onions for 5 minutes.
2. Add peanut butter, cayenne and curry powder and stir. Add bit water if needed. Sauté this for 2 more minutes.
3. Except for the kale, add remaining ingredients, cover with lid and switch on manual button for 8 minutes on high pressure.
4. When timer beeps, allow natural pressure release for

10-15 minutes. Set steam release handle to 'venting'. Open the lid.

5. Using an immersion blender, blend the soup until desired consistency.

6. Add chopped kale and stir again.

Lentil And Mixed Vegetable Soup

Preparation Time: 40 Minutes

Servings: 3

Ingredients:

- 1 cup green lentils
- 5 potatoes, chopped
- 2 celery ribs, chopped
- 2 carrots, chopped
- 1 yellow onion, chopped
- 2 bay leaves
- 1 can (14.5 fl ozof diced tomatoes
- 1 cup green peas (frozen or canned
- 1 cup kale or spinach, finely chopped (fresh or frozen
- 3½ cups water
- 2 tsp black pepper
- 3 garlic cloves, minced
- 2 tsp vegetable base (or use 2 cups water with 2 cups veggie broth

Directions:

1. Chop potatoes, celery, carrots, onion and mince garlic and add them to Instant Pot along with rest of ingredients except for green peas and kale or spinach.
2. Cover with lid and set iPot manual for 10 minutes over high pressure. Once done allow steam to release

naturally for about 15 minutes. Then release remaining steam using steam release handle. Open the lid.

3. Add green peas and kale or spinach. Stir the whole thing well. Let Instant Pot stay in 'Keep Warm' setting for around 10 minutes.

4. Remove bay leaves and serve the soup. When serving, add some salt or pepper to taste.

Turnip–Tomato Soup

Preparation Time: 15 minutes

Cooking Time: 33 minutes

Serving Size: 6

Ingredients:

- 1 tbsp butter
- 1 tbsp olive oil
- 1 large yellow onion, chopped
- 4 garlic cloves, minced
- 6 red bell peppers, deseeded and sliced
- 2 turnips, peeled and chopped
- 3 cups chopped tomatoes
- 4 cups vegetable stock
- Salt and freshly ground black pepper to taste
- 3 cups coconut milk
- 2 cups toasted chopped almonds
- 1 cup grated Parmesan cheese

Directions:

1. Over medium fire, heat butter and olive oil in a medium pot, and sauté onion and garlic until fragrant and soft, 3 minutes.
2. Stir in bell pepper and turnips; Cooking Time: until sweaty, 10 minutes.
3. Mix in tomatoes, vegetable stock, salt, and black

pepper. Cover lid and Cooking Time: over low heat for 20 minutes.

4. Turn heat off and using an immersion blender, puree ingredients until smooth. Stir in coconut milk.

5. Pour soup into serving bowls and garnish with almonds and Parmesan cheese.

6. Serve immediately with low carb cheese bread.

Nutrition:

Calories 955, Total Fat 86.65g, Total Carbs 10.5g, Fiber 6.5g, Net Carbs 4g, Protein 19.11g

Chilled Lemongrass And Avocado Soup

Preparation Time: 5 minutes

Cooking Time: 5 minutes + 1 hour refrigeration

Serving Size: 4

Ingredients:

- 2 stalks lemongrass, chopped
- 2 cups chopped avocado pulp
- 2 cups vegetable broth
- 2 lemons, juiced
- 3 tbsp chopped mint leaves + extra to garnish
- Salt and freshly ground black pepper to taste
- 2 cups heavy cream

Directions:

1. In a large pot, add lemongrass, avocado, and vegetable broth; bring to a slow boil over low heat until lemongrass softens and avocado warms through, 5 minutes.
2. Stir in lemon juice, mint leaves, salt, black pepper, and puree ingredients with an immersion blender.
3. Stir in heavy cream and turn heat off.
4. Dish soup into serving bowls, chill for 1 hour, and garnish with some mint leaves. Serve.

Nutrition:

Calories 339, Total Fat 33.3g, Total Carbs 6.58g, Fiber 3g, Net Carbs 3.58g, Protein 3.59g

Broccoli And Collard Soup

Preparation Time: 15 minutes

Cooking Time: 18 minutes

Serving Size: 4

Ingredients:

- 1 tbsp olive oil
- 2 tbsp butter
- 1 medium brown onion, thinly sliced
- 3 garlic cloves, finely sliced
- 1 large head broccoli, cut into florets
- 4 cups vegetable stock
- 2 cups collards
- ¼ cup freshly chopped parsley
- Salt and freshly ground black pepper to taste
- 1 tbsp fresh dill leaves for garnishing
- 1 cup grated Parmesan cheese for topping

Directions:

1. Over medium fire, heat olive oil and butter in a large saucepan and sauté onion and garlic until softened and fragrant, 3 minutes.
2. Stir in broccoli and Cooking Time: until softened, 5 minutes.
3. Add vegetable stock, salt, and black pepper. Cover pot and allow boiling. Reduce heat and simmer until

broccoli is very soft, 10 minutes.

4. Open lid and use an immersion blender to puree soup until completely smooth. Stir in collards, parsley, and adjust taste with salt and black pepper.

5. Dish soup, garnish with dill leaves and Parmesan cheese; serve warm.

Nutrition:

Calories 515, Total Fat 33.89g, Total Carbs 9.1g, Fiber 4.6g, Net Carbs 4.5g, Protein 38.33g

Pumpkin Stew

Preparation Time: 45 Minutes

Servings: 4

Ingredients:

- 21 oz sweet pumpkin, chopped
- 2 medium-sized onions, peeled and finely chopped
- 1 garlic clove
- 1 red pepper, finely chopped
- 1 tbsp of fresh tomato sauce
- ½ tbsp of chili powder
- 2 bay leaves
- 2 cups of red wine
- 1 cup of water
- 1 tsp of thyme, dry
- Salt and pepper to taste
- Oil for frying

Directions:

1. Plug in your instant pot and press "Sautee" button. Add chopped onions and stir-fry for 2 minutes. Add finely chopped red pepper, tomato sauce, and chili powder.
2. Continue to Cooking Time: until the pepper has softened.
3. Add the remaining ingredients and securely lock the lid. Adjust the steam release handle and set the timer for 8

minutes. Cooking Time: on high pressure.

4. When done, press "Cancel" button and release the steam naturally.

5. Enjoy!

Spring Vegetable Soup

Preparation Time: 8 minutes

Cooking Time: 12 minutes

Serving Size: 4

Ingredients:

- 4 cups vegetable stock
- 3 cups green beans, chopped
- 2 cups asparagus, chopped
- 1 cup pearl onions, peeled and halved
- 2 cups seaweed mix (or spinach
- 1 tbsp garlic powder
- Salt and freshly ground white pepper to taste
- 2 cups grated Parmesan cheese, for serving

Directions:

1. In a large pot, add vegetable stock, green beans, asparagus, and pearl onions. Season with garlic powder, salt and white pepper.
2. Cover pot and Cooking Time: over low heat until vegetables soften, 10 minutes.
3. Stir in seaweed mix and adjust taste with salt and white pepper.
4. Dish into serving bowls and top with plenty of Parmesan cheese.
5. Serve with low carb bread.

Nutrition:

Calories 196, Total Fat 11.9g, Total Carbs 10.02g, Fiber 5.7g, Net Carbs 4.32g

Bean Onion Stew

Preparation Time: 30 Minutes

Servings: 6

Ingredients:

- 1 pound of fresh beans
- 1 large onion, chopped
- 4 cloves of garlic, finely chopped
- 3 ½ oz of olives, pitted
- 1 tbsp of ginger powder
- 1 tbsp of turmeric
- 1 tbsp of salt
- 4 cups of water

Directions:

1. Plug in your instant pot and press "Sautee" button. Heat up the oil and add onions and garlic. Stir-fry for 5 minutes, or until onions translucent.
2. Now, add the remaining ingredients and close the lid. Press "Manual" button and set the timer for 15 minutes. Adjust the steam release and Cooking Time: on high pressure.
3. When done, press "Cancel" button and release the pressure naturally.
4. Open the pot and serve warm.
5. Enjoy!

SAUCES, AND CONDIMENTS

<u>Nacho Cheese Sauce</u>

Preparation time: 15 minutes

Cooking time: 5 minutes

Servings: 12

Ingredients:

- 2 cups cashews, unsalted , soaked in warm water for 15 minutes
- 2 teaspoons salt
- 1/2 cup nutritional yeast
- 1 teaspoon garlic powder
- 1/2 teaspoon smoked paprika
- 1/2 teaspoon red chili powder
- 1 teaspoon onion powder
- 2 teaspoons Sriracha
- 3 tablespoons lemon juice
- 4 cups water, divided

Directions:

1. Drain the cashews, transfer them to a food processor, then add remaining ingredients, reserving 3 cups water, and , and pulse for 3 minutes until smooth.

2. Tip the mixture in a saucepan, place it over medium heat and Cooking Time: for 3 to 5 minutes until the sauce has thickened and bubbling, whisking constantly.

3. When done, taste the sauce to adjust seasoning and then serve.

Nutrition Value:

Calories: 128 Cal

Fat: 10 g

Carbs: 8 g

Protein: 5 g

Fiber: 1 g

Thai Peanut Sauce

Preparation time: 10 minutes

Cooking time: 10 minutes

Servings: 4

Ingredients:

- 2 tablespoons ground peanut, and more for topping
- 2 tablespoons Thai red curry paste
- ½ teaspoon salt
- 1 tablespoon sugar
- 1/2 cup creamy peanut butter
- 2 tablespoons apple cider vinegar
- 3/4 cup coconut milk, unsweetened

Directions:

1. Take a saucepan, place it over low heat, add all the ingredients, whisk well until combined, and then bring the sauce to simmer.
2. Then remove the pan from heat, top with ground peanuts, and serve.

Nutrition Value:

Calories: 397 Cal

Fat: 50 g

Carbs: 16 g

Protein: 26 g

Fiber: 4 g

Garlic Alfredo Sauce

Preparation time: 10 minutes

Cooking time: 5 minutes

Servings: 4

Ingredients:

- 1 1/2 cups cashews, unsalted , soaked in warm water for 15 minutes
- 6 cloves of garlic, peeled, minced
- 1/2 medium sweet onion, peeled, chopped
- 1 teaspoon salt
- 1/4 cup nutritional yeast
- 1 tablespoon lemon juice
- 2 tablespoons olive oil
- 2 cups almond milk, unsweetened
- 12 ounces fettuccine pasta, cooked, for serving

Directions:

1. Take a small saucepan, place it over medium heat, add oil and when hot, add onion and garlic, and Cooking Time: for 5 minutes until sauté.

2. Meanwhile, drain the cashews, transfer them into a food processor, add remaining ingredients including onion mixture, except for pasta, and pulse for 3 minutes until very smooth.

3. Pour the prepared sauce over pasta, toss until coated and serve.

Nutrition Value:

Calories: 439 Cal

Fat: 20 g

Carbs: 52 g

Protein: 15 g

Fiber: 4 g

Cashew Yogurt

Preparation time: 12 hours and 5 minutes

Cooking time: 0 minute

Servings: 8

Ingredients:

- 3 probiotic supplements
- 2 2/3 cups cashews, unsalted , soaked in warm water for 15 minutes
- 1/4 teaspoon sea salt
- 4 tablespoon lemon juice
- 1 1/2 cup water

Directions:

1. Drain the cashews, add them into the food processor, then add remaining ingredients, except for probiotic supplements, and pulse for 2 minutes until smooth.
2. Tip the mixture in a bowl, add probiotic supplements, stir until mixed, then cover the bowl with a cheesecloth and let it stand for 12 hours in a dark and cool room.
3. Serve straight away.

Nutrition Value:

Calories: 252 Cal

Fat: 19.8 g

Carbs: 14.1 g

Protein: 8.3 g

Fiber: 1.5 g

SNACKS

Artichokes With Mayo Sauce

Preparation time: 10 minutes

Cooking time: 6 minutes

Total time: 16 minutes

Servings: 4

Ingredients:

- 2 artichokes, trimmed
- 1 tablespoon lemon juice
- 2 garlic cloves, minced
- A drizzle olive oil
- Sauce:
- 1 cup vegan mayonnaise
- ¼ cup olive oil
- ¼ cup coconut oil
- 3 garlic cloves

How to Prepare:

1. Toss artichokes with lemon juice, oil and 2 garlic cloves in a large bowl.
2. Place the seasoned artichokes in the air fryer basket and seal it.
3. Cooking Time: the artichokes for 6 minutes at 350 degrees on air fryer mode.

4. Blend coconut oil with olive oil, mayonnaise and 3 garlic cloves in a food processor.

5. Place the artichokes on the serving plates.

6. Pour the mayonnaise mixture over the artichokes.

7. Enjoy fresh.

Nutritional Values:

Calories 205

Total Fat 22.7 g

Saturated Fat 6.1 g

Cholesterol 4 mg

Sodium 227 mg

Total Carbs 26.1 g

Fiber 1.4 g

Sugar 0.9 g

Protein 5.2 g

Eggplant And Zucchini Snack

Preparation time: 10 minutes

Cooking time: 8 minutes

Total time: 18 minutes

Servings: 04

Ingredients:

- 1 eggplant, cubed
- 3 zucchinis, cubed
- 2 tablespoons lemon juice
- 1 teaspoon oregano, dried
- 3 tablespoons olive oil
- 1 teaspoon thyme, dried
- Salt and black pepper to taste

How to Prepare:

1. Take a baking dish suitable to fit in your air fryer.
2. Combine all ingredients in the baking dish.
3. Place the eggplant dish in the air fryer basket and seal it.
4. Cooking Time: them for 8 minutes at 360 degrees F on air fryer mode.
5. Enjoy warm.

Nutritional Values:

Calories 361

Total Fat 16.3 g

Saturated Fat 4.9 g

Cholesterol 114 mg

Sodium 515 mg

Total Carbs 29.3 g

Fiber 0.1 g

Sugar 18.2 g

Protein 3.3 g

Mushroom Stuffed Poblano

Preparation time: 10 minutes

Cooking time: 20 minutes

Total time: 30 minutes

Servings: 10

Ingredients:

- 10 poblano peppers, tops cut off and seeds removed
- 2 teaspoons garlic, minced
- 8 ounces mushrooms, chopped
- ½ cup cilantro, chopped
- 1 white onion, chopped
- 1 tablespoon olive oil
- Salt and black pepper to taste

How to Prepare:

1. Place a nonstick pan over medium heat and add oil.
2. Stir in mushrooms and onion, sauté for 5 minutes.
3. Add salt, black pepper, cilantro and garlic.
4. Stir while cooking for 2 additional minutes then take it off the heat.
5. Divide this mixture in the poblano peppers and stuff them neatly.
6. Place the peppers in the air fryer basket and seal it.
7. Cooking Time: them for 15 minutes at 350 degrees F on air fryer mode.

8. Enjoy.

Nutritional Values:

Calories 231

Total Fat 20.1 g

Saturated Fat 2.4 g

Cholesterol 110 mg

Sodium 941 mg

Total Carbs 20.1 g

Fiber 0.9 g

Sugar 1.4 g

Protein 4.6 g

Fried Mustard Greens

Preparation time: 10 minutes

Cooking time: 11 minutes

Total time: 21 minutes

Servings: 04

Ingredients:

- 2 garlic cloves, minced
- 1 tablespoon olive oil
- ½ cup yellow onion, sliced
- 3 tablespoons vegetable stock
- ¼ teaspoon dark sesame oil
- 1-pound mustard greens, torn
- salt and black pepper to the taste

How to Prepare:

1. Take a baking dish suitable to fit in your air fryer.
2. Add oil and place it over the medium heat and sauté onions in it for 5 minutes.
3. Stir in garlic, greens, salt, pepper, and stock.
4. Mix well then place the dish in the air fryer basket.
5. Seal it and Cooking Time: them for 6 minutes at 350 degrees F on air fryer mode.
6. Drizzle sesame oil over the greens.
7. Devour.

Nutritional Values:

Calories 201

Total Fat 8.9 g

Saturated Fat 4.5 g

Cholesterol 57 mg

Sodium 340 mg

Total Carbs 24.7 g

Fiber 1.2 g

Sugar 1.3 g

Protein 15.3 g

Cheese Brussels Sprouts

Preparation time: 10 minutes

Cooking time: 8 minutes

Total time: 18 minutes

Servings: 04

Ingredients:

- 1-pound brussels sprouts, washed
- 3 tablespoons vegan parmesan, grated
- Juice from 1 lemon
- 2 tablespoons vegan butter
- Salt and black pepper to the taste

How to Prepare:

1. Spread the brussels sprouts in the air fryer basket.
2. Seal it and Cooking Time: them for 8 minutes at 350 degrees F on air fryer mode.
3. Place a nonstick pan over medium high heat and add butter to melt.
4. Stir in pepper, salt, lemon juice, and brussels sprouts.
5. Mix well then add parmesan.
6. Serve warm.

Nutritional Values:

Calories 119

Total Fat 14 g

Saturated Fat 2 g

Cholesterol 65 mg

Sodium 269 mg

Total Carbs 19 g

Fiber 4 g

Sugar 6 g

Protein 5g

DESSERTS AND DRINKS

Peach Popsicles

Preparation time: 10 minutes

Cooking time: 2 hours

Total time: 2 hours and 10 minutes

Servings: 2

Ingredients:

- 2½ cups peaches, peeled and pitted
- 2 tablespoons agave
- ¾ cup coconut cream

How to Prepare:

1. In a blender, blend all the ingredients for popsicles until smooth.
2. Divide the popsicle blend into the popsicle molds.
3. Insert the popsicles sticks and close the molds.
4. Place the molds in the freezer for 2 hours to set.
5. Serve.

Nutritional Values:

Calories 231

Total Fat 20.1 g

Saturated Fat 2.4 g

Cholesterol 110 mg

Sodium 941 mg

Total Carbs 20.1 g

Fiber 0.9 g

Sugar 1.4 g

Protein 4.6 g

Protein Fat Bombs

Preparation time: 10 minutes

Cooking time: 1 hour

Total time: 1 hour and 10 minutes

Servings: 12

Ingredients:

- 1 cup coconut oil
- 1 cup peanut butter, melted
- ½ cup cocoa powder
- ¼ cup plant-based protein powder
- 1 pinch of salt
- 2 cups unsweetened shredded coconut

How to Prepare:

1. In a bowl, add all the ingredients except coconut shreds.
2. Mix well then make small balls out of this mixture and place them into silicone molds.
3. Freeze for 1 hour to set.
4. Roll the balls in the coconut shreds
5. Serve.

Nutritional Values:

Calories 293

Total Fat 16 g

Saturated Fat 2.3 g

Cholesterol 75 mg

Sodium 386 mg

Total Carbs 25.2 g

Sugar 2.6 g

Fiber 1.9 g

Protein 4.2 g

Coconut Fat Bombs

Preparation time: 10 minutes

Cooking time: 1 hour and 1 minute

Total time: 1 hour and 11 minutes

Servings: 12

Ingredients:

- 1 can coconut milk
- ¾ cup coconut oil
- 1 cup coconut flakes
- 20 drops liquid stevia

How to Prepare:

1. In a bowl combine all the ingredients.
2. Melt in a microwave for 1 minute.
3. Mix well then divide the mixture into silicone molds.
4. Freeze them for 1 hour to set.
5. Serve.

Nutritional Values:

Calories 119

Total Fat 14 g

Saturated Fat 2 g

Cholesterol 65 mg

Sodium 269 mg

Total Carbs 19 g

Fiber 4 g

Sugar 6 g

Protein 5g

Chocolate Peanut Fat Bombs

Preparation time: 10 minutes

Cooking time: 1 hour 1 minute

Total time: 1 hour and 11 minutes

Servings: 12

Ingredients:

- ½ cup coconut butter
- 1 cup plus 2 tablespoons peanut butter
- 5 tablespoons cocoa powder
- 2 teaspoons maple syrup

How to Prepare:

1. In a bowl, combine all the ingredients.
2. Melt them in the microwave for 1 minute.
3. Mix well then divide the mixture into silicone molds.
4. Freeze them for 1 hour to set.
5. Serve.

Nutritional Values:

Calories 246

Total Fat 7.4 g

Saturated Fat 4.6 g

Cholesterol 105 mg

Sodium 353 mg

Total Carbs 29.4 g

Sugar 6.5 g

Fiber 2.7 g

Protein 7.2 g

Apple Pie Bites

Preparation time: 10 minutes

Cooking time: 1 hour

Total time: 1 hour and 10 minutes

Servings: 12

Ingredients:

- 1 cup walnuts, chopped
- ½ cup coconut oil
- ¼ cup ground flax seeds
- ½ ounce freeze dried apples
- 1 teaspoon vanilla extract
- 1 teaspoon cinnamon
- Liquid stevia, to taste

How to Prepare:

1. In a bowl add all the ingredients.
2. Mix well then roll the mixture into small balls.
3. Freeze them for 1 hour to set.
4. Serve.

Nutritional Values:

Calories 211

Total Fat 25.5 g

Saturated Fat 12.4 g

Cholesterol 69 mg

Sodium 58 mg

Total Carbs 32.4 g

Fiber 0.7 g

Sugar 0.3 g

Protein 1.4 g

Mojito Fat Bombs

Preparation time: 10 minutes

Cooking time: 1 hour and 1 minute

Total time: 1 hour and 11 minutes

Servings: 12

Ingredients:

- ¾ cup hulled hemp seeds
- ½ cup coconut oil
- 1 cup fresh mint
- ½ teaspoon mint extract
- Juice & zest of two limes
- ¼ teaspoon stevia

How to Prepare:

1. In a bowl, combine all the ingredients.
2. Melt in the microwave for 1 minute.
3. Mix well then divide the mixture into silicone molds.
4. Freeze them for 1 hour to set.
5. Serve.

Nutritional Values:

Calories 319

Total Fat 10.6 g

Saturated Fat 3.1 g

Cholesterol 131 mg

Sodium 834 mg

Total Carbs 31.4 g

Fiber 0.2 g

Sugar 0.3 g

Protein 4.6 g

Lightning Source UK Ltd.
Milton Keynes UK
UKHW020728010321
379576UK00001B/32